How to turn Stumbling Blocks into

STEPPIN

Using the Creative Advantage
in Personal Evangelism

MW01166649

──────────────── **CONTENTS** ────────────────

Published by:
Agape Ministries Ltd.
Fairgate House, Kings Road
Tyseley, Birmingham
B11 2AA
Tel: 0121 765 4404
Fax: 0121 765 4065

Scripture quotations from The Holy Bible New International Version © 1973, 1978, 1984 International Bible Society. Published by Hodder and Stoughton and used by permission.

Stepping Stones
August 2002

This publication is an updated version of the original publication *Turning the Tables in Witnessing*.

ISBN 0 948860 09 X

Introduction

T he gospel always demands decision. Questions and objections are often raised in order to avoid this challenge. They present themselves as stumbling blocks, as reasons why "I couldn't possibly believe that." But, handled carefully you can turn them into stepping stones. Not avoiding the issues, but dealing with them in such a way that you can move on to make clear the positive challenge of the gospel.

This booklet aims to give you basic answers to some common stumbling blocks to the Christian faith. The answers are brief so that you can easily remember them and use them in discussion. There are a number of other books that are more comprehensive, but we want to give you concise and helpful responses that you can use at those crucial moments in a conversation.

Objections tend to drive us back into a defensive position. The New Testament commands us to "give the reason for the hope that you have" (1 Peter 3:15), but we do not want to get stuck in that defensive stance. We need to take the initiative and focus attention once again on the challenge of the gospel. This booklet will help you do just that.

But a word of warning. No one is won into the Kingdom of God by being beaten in an argument. These tools are not designed for you to demonstrate your intellectual superiority. We are out to win people, not discussions. Nor are we trying simply to prove to ourselves that we are right. Our aim at all times must be to show not only that Christianity is reasonable, but that we care about the person we are talking to.

So, some suggestions:

❖ Depend on the Holy Spirit to illuminate people's minds through the Word of God. "After I share Christ with someone who has honest doubts, I give him enough evidences to answer his questions or satisfy his curiosity and then turn the conversation back to his relationship to Christ. The presentation of evidence should never be a substitute for using the Word of God." Josh McDowell[1]

❖ Love the person you are talking to and assure them often that you want the best for them. Make it clear that you are not simply out to win the argument.

❖ Listen carefully to what they have to say and ask yourself "Why is this question bothering them?" Be encouraging about any interest they have. You could begin by saying, "I am interested you said that; you have obviously been thinking about these things." Encourage them to pray, "O God, I want to know the truth. I am trusting you to help me find it."

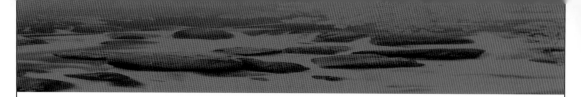

❖ Don't be afraid to admit when you do not know the answer to a question. This adds greater force to what you do know!

❖ Keep refocusing the discussion on Jesus Christ. People should be drawn magnetically to him rather than bowled out intellectually by one or two fast balls from you. All good discussion comes back to Jesus Christ as the centre.

❖ Use the "Knowing God Personally" booklet[2] as a means of making the challenge clear. If you have gone through it with your friend already, refer back to it in your answer, relating their question to the relevant point to show how that aspect of the Gospel answers that objection. Because a person has heard it once does not mean that they have grasped it. They will be helped to see both the wide range of Gospel truths and also the inner logic by which one truth leads on to another.

❖ Point out that Christian faith is based on facts. It is not a leap into the dark, or an irrational optimism, but a well thought out step based on the evidence of history and scripture focused on Jesus Christ. Challenge people to face the force of that evidence and take that step.

Throughout "Stepping Stones" reference is made to the evangelistic booklet "Knowing God Personally". This is an effective tool that you can use in evangelistic presentations. (The text of this booklet is included in the appendix.) Links are suggested for moving from a stumbling block and stepping back to the key issues.

You will not master all the material in "Stepping Stones" by reading it once or twice. Study each section carefully by yourself or in a group, mastering the main points. Think through how you could explain it to someone else in a natural way. Then, after you have discussed one of these topics in an evangelistic conversation, refer back to the outline given in this booklet and see where you could improve on what you said. Make your own notes in the margin and see where you can improve on this booklet too!

The Stumbling Block

The question challenges the justice and the love of God. "Why does God condemn someone for not believing in Jesus Christ when they have never heard of Him? Are we not saved by our sincere efforts? If we are 'good' pagans, is God not just as pleased?"

An Initial Challenge

"That's an interesting question. But there is another question which is closely related to it: What about those who **have** heard and have done nothing about it? I think that is the real issue."

The Biblical Attitude

God reveals himself to **all** people in two ways:

Nature. The world around us with its order and intricacy, from the vast universe down to the minute atom, points beyond itself to a Mind that made it. The probability of it happening by chance is similar to that of a thousand monkeys typing for a thousand years and producing a sonnet of Shakespeare.

"For since the creation of the world God's invisible qualities - his eternal power and divine nature - have been clearly seen, being understood from what has been made, so that men are without any excuse."   Romans 1:20

Many philosophies today recognise the power, order and beauty that there is in the natural world, and make "Nature" into a god to be revered and worshipped. Yet such order and beauty clearly beg the question, "How could this all have come about just by chance?" Does it not make more sense to worship the Creator rather than what he has created?

Conscience. Humans, unlike any other creatures, have a sense of "ought to" which conflicts with their "want to."

"Indeed, when Gentiles, who do not have the law, do by nature things required by the law... they show that the requirements of the law are written on their hearts, their consciences also bearing witness."   Romans 2:14,15

We may choose to go against our conscience, but we can never wholly escape it. What has made us that way? What has made us different from all other creatures?

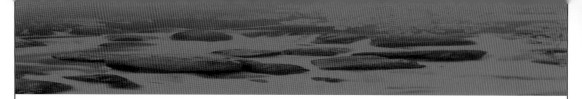

God reveals himself to **some** people in one supreme way: **Jesus Christ**. He is the climax of God's revelation.

"No one has ever seen God, but the only Son, who is at the Father's side, has made him known."

John 1:18

He is visible proof of the depth of God's love to all people.

God judges a person on three counts:

1 **Did they worship?** In response to the revelation in nature which they had, did they worship the one true God?

2 **Did they obey?** In response to the revelation in conscience which they had, did they sincerely obey God's commands?

3 **Would they have trusted Christ if they had heard?** God bases his judgement on what would have happened if someone had heard the gospel. It is part of his omniscience to know not only what will happen, but also what would happen if a different set of circumstances were to occur. Jesus states this clearly in Matthew 11:21-22:

"Woe to you, Korazin! Woe to you, Bethsaida! If the miracles that were performed in you had been performed in Tyre and Sidon, they would have repented long ago in sackcloth and ashes. But I tell you, if will be more bearable for Tyre and Sidon on the day of judgement than for you."

Korazin and Bethsaida were towns in Galilee where he had preached and done miracles. They remained hard and unrepentant. But he knew that the pagan cities of Tyre and Sidon would have responded differently given the opportunity. This would be taken into account on the day of judgement.

God gets no pleasure out of condemning a person.

"For I take no pleasure in the death of anyone, declares the Sovereign Lord. Repent and live!

(Ezekiel 18:32)

He also will judge Christians for the failure to carry the good news to everyone.

The Stepping Stone

"You yourself **have** heard. God will assess you on the basis of what you know about Jesus Christ and what response you have made to him. Let me show you what God expects." Go through the "Knowing God Personally" booklet emphasising the transition between Point Three and Four: "It is not enough just to know these facts... We must receive Jesus Christ into our lives as Saviour and Lord."

The Stumbling Block

The questioner is concerned with being broad-minded and tolerant. The implication is, first, that God is rather arbitrary and unfair if be insists on just one way to himself. Second, that you are being dogmatic and bigoted in your beliefs. Today's thinking emphasises that:

✦ Conviction is too aggressive and commitment is too rigid.

✦ Ambivalence is better than being convinced of the truth.

✦ An individual can make their own way to God if they are sufficiently sincere and determined.

✦ It is important to allow every individual the right to do things their way.

✦ No one individual's path to God is any more valid or correct than another's.

✦ Truth is relative.

Such attitudes remove the need to make rational, and sometimes hard, choices that involve becoming committed to a certain path. It allows people to believe everything and nothing.

An Initial Challenge

"I am interested that you should say that because it shows you have been thinking about these things. In what way would you say they all lead to God?"

Wait for their answer, which will probably point to the common emphasis on sincerity and moral conduct.

"It would be nice to believe that there are many ways to God, but if you examine what the different religions say, you will find that there are many significant areas in which they say contradictory things. They cannot all be right. To claim that they all lead to God means that, in these significant areas, you are saying that they must all be wrong. You would have to throw out the vast body of each religion's teaching in order to be left with those areas in which they agree. That is hardly being tolerant and could be taken as an insult to anyone who follows a religion. The facts of the matter cause me to believe that the Christian way stands out from the rest."

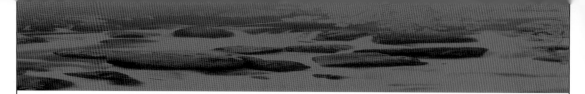

The Biblical Attitude

God cares about all people. He has *"not left himself without witness"* among the nations (Act 14:17). Christians do not have a monopoly on the truth. God is quite capable of revealing truth to anyone (Acts 17:28, Romans 1:19) and they are quite capable of responding to it (Romans 2:14f). Also, God does not have favourites or show partiality (Acts 10:34-35). He wants everyone to come to him (2 Peter 3:9).

Yet there are distinct differences between what Christ taught and what other religions say. Other religions put the emphasis on man's efforts to reach up to God (or gods). Christ put the emphasis on a personal, loving, just God who has made a supreme effort to reach out to mankind and rescue us from the mess we have made of the world.

The crucial issue is what do we make of Christ? If he is the one true God in human form, then it is patently clear that no-one can be ranked with him and we must take his teachings as the final authority on what God requires. Only that teaching which agrees with his own can be taken as valid.

Of course, there are many overlaps between Jesus' moral teachings and those of other religions. But it is also worth noting that Jesus goes considerably beyond what most other religions teach.

If Christ is **not** the one true God, then he has no such claim to uniqueness, there can be no standard against which to measure each religion, and we must treat all "revelations" on the same level.

So, before we can legitimately go down the path of seeing all religions as being equal, we must address the issue of the identity of Christ. We should be clear that it is Christ and not the Christian religions for which final authority is claimed. We are not claiming the superiority of Christians over the members of other religions, but that God has acted in history in the person of Christ and it is therefore to him that we must look for the answer to the way to God.

(At this point you may need to refer to Section 8 on the identity of Christ)

The Stepping Stone

"If Jesus Christ is God, then his teaching is the one we should follow most closely. The Knowing God Personally booklet, especially Point Three, points to his uniqueness and the way you can receive him personally."

"The resurrection did not really happen"

The Stumbling Block

The questioner has two problems in mind:

✦ The New Testament story is unreliable.

✦ Miracles are hard to accept in a scientific age.

The first problem can be answered from Section 5. The second demands an historical study of the facts without any assumption as to wheather miracles do or do not happen.

An Initial Challenge

"I am interested that you should say that. You have obviously been thinking about these things. What makes you come to that conclusion? Have you ever investigated the evidence?"

The Biblical Basis

What happened? Four facts:

1 **The prophecy of Jesus.** Jesus said in advance that he would rise again three days after his death (Luke 18:31-33). But the disciples did not believe him at all (Luke 18:34).

2 **The empty tomb**. The tomb was empty (Matthew 28:6), even though heavily guarded (Matthew 27:62-66). Anyone in Jerusalem could visit it in order to see for himself.

3 **The appearances of Jesus**. Jesus appeared to his disciples in a variety of situations, e.g. in the upper room, on the road to Emmaus. These various records of Jesus' appearances answer the questions that any court of law would ask: Was there an eye-witness? Were there a number of such witnesses? Do their stories agree? Do their stories differ in perspective?

4 **The changed disciples**. Within seven weeks the disciples were turned from beaten men into world revolutionaries, described by a jealous mob as *"these men who have caused trouble all over the world"* (Acts 17:6). A great effect demands a great cause.

Who took the body? Four inadequate explanations:

1 **The Romans?** They wanted to close the whole affair. Pontius Pilate washed his hands of all responsibility. The body was of no value to them.

2 **The Jews?** They put a guard on the tomb. Later they must have moved heaven and earth to find the body of Jesus and suppress this Christian story of resurrection.

3 **The Disciples?** "They invented the whole thing." But soon they suffered terribly for their "fiction." People give up their deceptions when they became unprofitable.

4 **The Disciples?** "They were fooled by hallucinations." Psychologists tell us that hallucinations depend upon a spirit of positive expectancy; but on the contrary the disciples were convinced that everything was finished. This was not just wishful thinking. In addition, Jesus' appearances were very solid (not "ghost-like") and came in a wide variety of circumstances.

The only explanation to fit the facts is that God raised Jesus Christ from the dead and that he is truly alive.

Illustration

Many people have set out to prove that the resurrection never happened. One was a lawyer, Frank Morison, who wrote the well-known book "Who Moved the Stone?"[3] His first chapter is entitled, "The Book that Would Not be Written." In it he says that he set out to write a book to prove that Jesus never rose again. But the facts compelled him to reverse his convictions. Instead he wrote his book to argue that Jesus must have risen from the dead.

Stepping Stone

"If Jesus really rose again, as he predicted, then he must be who he claimed to be and we should take seriously all that he said. He claimed to be God's answer to your need. There is nothing more important than your relationship to him. Let us look at the Third Point of the 'Knowing God Personally' booklet which deals with this."

"I don't believe in God"

The Stumbling Block

There is an over-confidence that says, "because I cannot see or feel God, I do not believe in him. Things are true and real only if I can prove them scientifically." Or it may be a way of saying, "I don't want to believe."

An Initial Challenge

"I am interested you should say that. Why is that? How can you be sure that God does not exist? No one has total information. How much of the world's knowledge do you possess? Couldn't it be possible that God exists outside of your realm of knowledge?"

The Biblical Approach

The Bible nowhere sets out **proofs** of God's existence on the lines of 2+2=4. But it provides a number of "signposts to God", aspects of the world which point irresistibly to him. Taken one by one they are not conclusive, but put together they are compelling. Some of these are:

1 **Nature**. (Romans 1:19-20) The world around us presents us with order and law in the minuteness of the atom and the vastness of the universe. Wherever in human experience we see order, for instance trees in a straight line, we say "Someone put them that way." Listen to how often naturalists like David Attenborough talk about "design" of nature. Design demands a designer. The world does not explain itself.

2 **Conscience**. Humans, unlike any other creature, have a sense of "ought to" which often conflicts with their "want to" (Romans 2:14-15). Why?

3 **Jesus Christ**. His unique character, death and resurrection can only be explained by his being more than a man. He is the supreme signpost to the supernatural. See section 8 for the expansion of this idea.

4 **Prophecy**. With the Bible there is a unique pattern of prophecy and its detailed fulfilment that only a supernatural Mind could have worked out. Jesus Christ himself fulfilled over three hundred of these prophecies, including where he would be born, who his parents would be, how he would die and where he would be buried. These were not fulfilled by conscious planning.

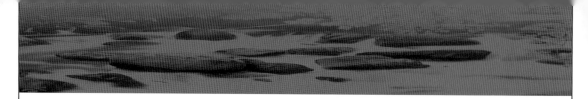

5 **Desire for meaning**. If you leave God out and think logically, this world is pointless - just a product of chance and evolution. As Bertrand Russell put it: "We must build our lives on the foundations of unyielding despair."[4] Why, then, do we long for meaning and purpose? If we are only the product of a meaningless world, why are we not content to live a meaningless life? Something else has made us like this: this world does not explain it. The existence of God is essential if the world is to make sense.

The Stepping Stone

God does not become a living reality to us until we make a step of personal commitment. Turn to Point Four of "Knowing God Personally" to make this point clear. You could add your own testimony by saying "Let me tell you how God became real in my life."

"I don't believe the Bible"

The Stumbling Block

Modern secular thought has thrown so much doubt on the reliability of the Bible that many people have been brainwashed into considering it contradictory and anti-scientific. People captured by this viewpoint need to know the facts.

An Initial Challenge

"I am interested that you should say that. But before a person rejects the Bible they should know what its central message is. What would you say that is?" Wait for them to answer. You can continue, "I would like to show you how strong the evidence is for its central character, Jesus Christ. People accept all the other characters of ancient history on much less evidence. But they try to debunk the story of Jesus because they don't want it to be true."

The Biblical Basis

There are five important points to be made:

1 The New Testament writers got their facts straight

They were very careful to be accurate, checking their sources and giving eye-witness accounts.

Luke - did thorough research (Luke 1:1-4), visiting people who saw and lived with Jesus.

John - emphasised that his gospel is an eye-witness account (John 19:35).

Paul - listed the witnesses of the resurrection so that people could check for themselves (1 Corinthians 15:4-8).

Sir William Ramsey, a leading 20th-century historian, was doubtful for some time about Luke's accuracy. But archaeology and careful research convinced him. The gospel writers weren't trying to write biographies of Jesus, but that doesn't mean that their work was not historical. Historical fiction is a modern invention and was completely unknown in the ancient world. Anyway, who could have invented Jesus? As has been said "It would take a Jesus to invent a Jesus." (David Strauss).[5]

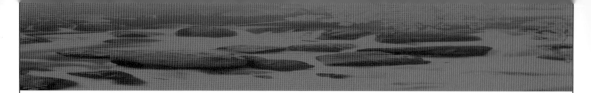

2 The disciples did not exaggerate about Jesus

It is sometimes said that the followers of Jesus turned this great and admired teacher into a supernatural Son of God, in the way that happens in folklore. But notice that they were Jews whose whole way of thought and upbringing would have been completely against this. For thousands of years Jews had died rather than bow to anyone but God. Paul was a Pharisee of the Pharisees. It can only have been the overwhelming evidence of Jesus himself that forced them to acknowledge him as God.

3 The record has been preserved accurately

Books were handwritten in those days on parchment or reed paper (papyrus) which were copied again and again. "The evidence for the text of the books of the New Testament is better than for any other ancient book. This is true both in the number of surviving manuscripts and in the nearness of the date of some of these manuscripts to the date when the book was originally written." (From the Preface to the Holy Bible - Revised Standard Version).[6]

4 There is good support from outside the Bible

✦ **Josephus**, a Jew and friend of the emperor, recorded the important facts about the life of Jesus when he wrote his "History of the Jews" in 90 A.D.

✦ **Thallus**, a non-Christian, writing in 52 A.D. mentioned that the darkness over all the earth at the time of the crucifixion was seen in Rome.

✦ **Seutonius**, the official historian of the Ceasars, wrote: "As the Jews were making constant disturbances at the instigation of Christ (*"Chrestus"*) he (Cladius) expelled them from Rome."

5 The Bible shows extraordinary unity

Considering that the Bible was written over a period of 1600 years, by 40 separate authors ranging from kings to fishermen, in places extending from Italy to Iran - it shows extraordinary unity.

The Stepping Stone

"These are facts of history. They make a strong foundation for the life, death and resurrection of Jesus Christ. There is only one more question to be answered, "What will you do with Jesus?" There is only one answer: "We must receive Jesus Christ into our lives as Saviour and Lord." Continue with Point Four of the "Knowing God Personally" booklet.

The Stumbling Block

The Spanish Inquisition, the persecution of the Jews, the conflict of Protestants and Catholics in Northern Ireland, etc. all make people ask, "What difference does Christianity make in people's lives?" Possibly the questioner has had some unhappy experiences in a church or with a Christian. Or they may feel morally superior, "I could never behave like that", never realising the depths of self-centredness revealed in every one of us when we are under pressure.

An Initial Challenge

"I am interested you should say that. What specifically do you have in mind? This problem shows that there is a tremendous difference between religion and real Christianity."

The Biblical Approach

The New Testament emphasises that:

✦ Our loyalty is to Jesus Christ and his perfect example, not to his imperfect followers. For a vivid contrast between the attitude of Jesus and that of his disciples, look at Luke 9:51-56.

✦ There is an enormous difference between an involvement with institutional Christianity and a personal relationship with Christ. A true believer (one whom Christ indwells) will have a genuine love and concern for those around him (1 John 4:20).

✦ When people become Christians they do not become perfect, they remain in need of forgiveness. The difference is that they have found the source of that forgiveness and the power to change.

Outside the Bible

During 2000 years, no other body of people has such a record of service to humanity as the Christian Church. But as usual, the bad things have hit the headlines of history. So much good passes unnoticed.

Christians have had the initiative in bringing about the following changes.

- ✦ Prison Reforms
- ✦ Child Work Laws
- ✦ Abolition of Slavery
- ✦ Development of Hospitals
- ✦ AIDS Hospices

- ✦ The Red Cross
- ✦ The Humane Society
- ✦ Orphanages
- ✦ Public Education

Malcolm Muggeridge reported that in his travels to remote parts of the world he had found many schools and hospitals run by Christians, but none by humanists.[7]

The Stepping Stone

Tell the stories of two or three people you know whose lives have been changed by the Lord. Give your own testimony. Then, in the Knowing God Personally booklet, point to the transition and the end of the Third Point: "It is not enough just to know these facts... We must receive Jesus Christ into our lives as Saviour and Lord." This is where many religious people have missed out.

"Religion is just a crutch for the weak" or "I can manage without God"

The Stumbling Block

The objection expresses a basic human drive to be self-sufficient, independent of God and able to take care of oneself in life's deepest problems. People fear that they will lose their personal identity and freedom. They have an exaggerated idea of their own ability and are blind to their needs and sin.

An Initial Challenge

"There is something inside each of us that wants to be utterly self-sufficient. But Christians are honest. They know that they need strength for living from beyond themselves. Everyone does this in practice - cigarettes, beer, sex, drugs, another person, image, power, money. But they are not honest enough to admit it - or to see that all these human crutches will break sooner or later. Only the Christian's "crutch", Jesus Christ, will last forever."

The Biblical Approach

1 Without God we are incomplete

God made us to function on all levels of our personality - body, mind and spirit. In fact without God we are "not all there." We were made with a spiritual side to our nature, for contact with God and the spiritual world (1 Thessalonians 5:23). But for so many this side of their nature is ignored in the pressure of life, as was done by the rich fool in Jesus' parable (Luke 12:16-21). The reason for this is that they are "dead towards God." The spiritual aspect of their personalities is switched off by sin and rebellion (Ephesians 2:1-3). The person who says they can do without God is only two thirds alive, satisfied with less than the best that life has to offer. Whether they realise it or not, they are missing out.

2 Our initial rebellion

From the beginning people have been trying to get away from God and find sufficiency and all the answers in themselves. In Genesis 3, mankind's temptation was to strike out in independence of God. One of the reasons they ate the fruit of the tree of the knowledge of good and evil was to enable them to *"be like God, knowing good and evil"* (Genesis 3:5), independent and self-sufficient. This independence was not God's plan for them.

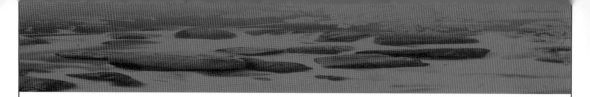

3 Jesus Christ depended totally on God

The one perfect human being, Jesus Christ, depended on God more than anyone else. As the second person of the trinity he could have acted in total self-sufficiency. Yet he depended on God completely. *"The Son can do nothing by himself"* (John 5:19). To trust in God like this does not make you a personality cripple, but makes you alive in all areas of your being, making you more and more like Jesus Christ.

The Stepping Stone

"Let me show you how you can become a complete person, fully alive to God at every level." Continue by using the Knowing God Personally booklet, showing God's love, our need and God's provision in Jesus Christ for our failure.

"Jesus was just a great man"

The Stumbling Block

Two thoughts lie behind this assertion:

✦ Jesus was a man who was later idealised by his followers - like the hero in a folk-tale.

✦ The most basic is that there is no God or supernatural.

A study of the claims, character and actions of Jesus Christ provides some of the best evidence for the existence of God.

An Initial Challenge

"I am interested you should say that. Many people say the same as you, but could you prove from the evidence that Jesus was only a man? The evidence for the deity of Jesus must have been overwhelmingly convincing to change the minds of his staunchly monotheistic disciples."

The Biblical Basis

The facts of history show that Jesus is in a class of his own and is far more than "just a great man." Unlike Mohammed, Buddha, Confucius and other founders of religions:

1 **Only he was foretold in detail centuries before he came** (Matthew 1:22-23). It was prophesied where he would be born, who his parents would be, how he would live and die and rise again. When King Herod asked the teachers of the law to check the prophecies about the Messiah's birth, they were able to tell him where to look for Jesus (Matthew 2:3-6). He fulfilled over three hundred prophecies in detail. This is unique in the world's history and literature.

2 **Only he said he came from outside the world** (John 6:38) Others claimed messages, revelations, insights, but none claimed to come from outside this world.

3 **Only he said he was without flaw of character** (John 8:46) and backed it up by the way he lived. It is a characteristic of saints and spiritual leaders that the more they develop the more conscious they become of their ignorance and shortcomings. Jesus was never like this.

4 **Only he declared he was God** (John 5:18; 8:58; 10:33) and backed it up by a life of wisdom, authority, humility and love.

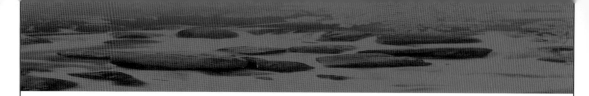

5 **Only he died for the sin of the world,** the result of our rebellion against God. Other people just died. Jesus Christ was born to die (Mark 10:45).

6 **Only he rose from the grave** as he promised he would (Luke 24:33-35). You can visit the tomb of Mohammed; his bones are there. Buddha was cremated, his ashes were buried in ten centres in India.

Was he a LIAR?
People lie for profit. When the lie is unprofitable, when death threatens, they confess. Jesus confessed nothing. Further, people lie because they are selfish. But every aspect of Jesus' personality shows how selfless he was.

Was he a LUNATIC?
Schizophrenia is a symptom of a disturbed personality. But in every way Jesus displays balance, humility, poise and selflessness. He does not have the marks of mental illness or megalomania. He came to serve. He came to give his life. He even washed the feet of the disciples, including the traitor, Judas.

Conclusion:
The explanation that he was Lord is the only one that really fits the facts.

Quotation

"A man who was merely a man and said the things Jesus said would not be a great moral teacher. He would either be a lunatic - on a level with the man who says he is a poached egg - or else he would be the Devil of Hell. You must make your choice. Either this man was and is the Son of God: or else a madman or something worse. You can shut him up for a fool, you can spit at him and kill him as a demon; or you can fall at his feet and call him Lord and God. But let us not come with any patronising nonsense about his being a great human teacher. He has not left that open to us. He did not intend to."

C.S. Lewis, Mere Christianity[8]

The Stepping Stone

"If Jesus Christ is God, then nothing is more important than your relationship to him. He is Lord. The Knowing God Personally booklet, especially Point Three, shows his uniqueness and the way you can receive him personally".

"All the suffering in the world shows that God is not good"

The Stumbling Block

Pain, bereavement, natural tragedies and war raise profound questions that cause much personal anguish. The questioner may have several thoughts in mind:

✦ Is God fair to let this happen to me?

✦ If the world is so random, is there a God at all?

✦ If God is love, why does he not do something about the world's suffering?

This objection is an attack on the justice, the love and sometimes the existence of God. In fact, modern men and women have put God on trial and asked him to justify himself for creating such a painful world.

An Initial Challenge

"I am interested that you said that. Is there perhaps some experience that you have had that has caused you to doubt that there is a God of love? I do not have any quick and easy answers to the problem of suffering. I don't fully understand why some people suffer so much, but I do know that God cares. In fact he cares so much that he was prepared to become a human being himself and suffer with human beings and at the hands of human beings."

The Biblical Attitude

✦ **Is suffering related to sinning?** Yes and no. Suffering is not necessarily the consequence of an individual's sin but rather of our general rebellion towards God. The sin of one person may cause innocent individuals to suffer (Romans 5:12). We get involved in suffering as part of being born into a sinful world.

✦ **Does God care?** God is not distant, totally detached from the world he created and its pain. He became a human being and experienced the full depth of human suffering - its anguish, weakness, bitterness, desolation and death. "He took up our infirmities and carried our diseases" (Matthew 8:17). We cannot explain everything about God's attitude towards pain, but we can be sure of his love. *"But God demonstrates his own love for us in this: While we were still sinners, Christ died for us"* (Romans 5:8). God is not a careless spectator.

✦ **Can God do anything about suffering?** Yes, the Bible does not explain in detail why there is suffering. It does tell us how it can be overcome. The Bible is essentially a practical book. After the Cross comes the Resurrection. God can and does work miracles of healing. God is able to take suffering that is given to him, turn it around and make it a source of blessing to us and to others. His grace is sufficient (2 Corinthians 12:9), and enables us to face the problem.

The Bible also explains, in the book of Job, that an individual's suffering may not at all be the result of their own personal sin.

A Practical Suggestion

It is easy to theorise glibly on this problem of pain, especially when one has not suffered deeply oneself. The best way to help someone is to show them God's way in action. Tell them the story of a friend you know who has overcome suffering through faith in Christ. Or lend them a book such as "To Live Again" by Catherine Marshall[9], describing the death of her husband.

The Stepping Stone

"So much human suffering is caused by humanity's sin against God and fellow human beings. This is shown in Point Two of the Knowing God Personally booklet. The proof of God's concern is clearly set out on Point Three with its focus on the cross." We need to point out that the deepest suffering is our sin and separation from God. "God in his grace has dealt with that at the expense of the total sacrifice of himself. It only remains for us to begin the solution by accepting Jesus Christ ourselves."

"I have always done my best"

The Stumbling Block

Behind this objection, and also a number of related ones, lies the idea that God accepts us on the basis of our merits and achievements. That he operates a productivity bonus which goes to those who have been sincere and lived decently. The idea of "self-justification" is written deeply into all human nature in its rebellion against God. It crops up from the beginning to the end of the Bible as the most dangerous attitude anyone can have towards God.

An Initial Challenge

"I am interested you should say that. Have you ever felt you could have done better? That you have not lived up to what God intended you to be? I am sure that everyone of us would admit that we sometimes feel this way. There are times when we have deliberately chosen the selfish way."

The Biblical Teaching

✦ God measures us against Jesus Christ, not against other people. Jesus is the perfect person. We may say "I have done as well as anybody else." Some have got closer to God's standard than others, but all fall short.

✦ God judges thoughts as well as actions. "But I say to you that everyone who looks at a woman lustfully has already committed adultery with her in his heart." (Matthew 5:28)

✦ God judges us not only by how we treated our fellow human beings. The first and great commandment is "Love the Lord your God with all your heart and with all your soul and with all your mind and with all your strength" (Mark 12:30). **The first thing** he looks at is whether we have given him this pride of place in our lives. Then secondly he looks at our obedience to the second commandment: "Love your neighbour as yourself" (Mark 12:31)

An Illustration

Many people think of God as if he had a giant ledger in heaven. Every person has a debit page and a credit page. Without any difficulty we get a lot of sins recorded on the debit side. We feel that the aim of our efforts is to accumulate as much as possible on the credit side by good living. Then hopefully we will end life with a credit balance and God will welcome us to Heaven. Fallacy: We can never do enough to balance the account and even if we could, that does not atone for the wrong done.

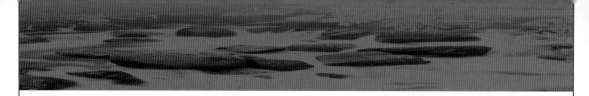

There is only one way out of the hopeless debt. Christ must pay for everything and then the debit page will be wiped clean. *"This is my blood of the covenant, which is poured out for many for the forgiveness of sins"* (Matthew 26:28).

The Stepping Stone

Refer to the Knowing God Personally booklet. Point Two explains clearly that by our own efforts we can never reach God. Point Three shows Jesus Christ as God's provision for our sin.

Probing the weaknesses

As well as dealing with questions and objections that are put to us, an important part of evangelism is helping the person to recognise the weaknesses in their own thinking that keeps them from seeing the truth of the gospel.

We are not trying to score points in a debate. We are aiming in love to show a person the depth of their need for Jesus Christ. Presenting him is the main purpose of all our discussion. Within this overall aim, we may need to undermine the arguments of those opposed as well as to answer their objections.

1 "Your unbelief could be as psychological as my belief"

Freud, the pioneer psychologist, wrote a book on religion entitled "The Future of an Illusion."[10] Belief in God, he said, is the product of our needs. As children depend on their father, so adults need a big Father figure in the sky. Conclusion: Belief is psychological.

However, this argument rebounds. Unbelief also is psychological. Rejection of God is due to rejection of, or rebellion against, parents. Refusal to believe is usually not on rational grounds. Aldous Huxley, a prominent atheist, wrote: "I had motives for not wanting the world to have a meaning; and consequently assumed that it had none, and was able without difficulty to find satisfying reasons for this assumption...For myself, the philosophy of meaninglessness was essentially an instrument of liberation, sexual and political."[11]

The unbeliever likes to think that they are more rational or scientific than the believer. They are not. Often they are not so much an unbeliever as a won't believer. "Now let us look at the solid facts and evidence of Jesus Christ."

2 "It is the non-Christian, not the Christian, who is really running away from life"

Christians are sometimes accused of using their faith as an escape from life's pressures. But if people are refusing to face up to the claims of the gospel, it is they who are running away. You may help get this across by asking your hearer:

✦ Are you running away from the facts of the life, death and ressurection of Jesus Christ - solid facts of history which cannot be avoided and must be explained somehow? Their obvious meaning has revolutionary consequences today.

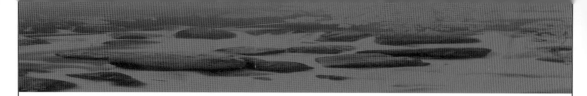

+ Are you running away from facing humankind's deepest problems: self-centredness and guilt before God? In fact, you may be avoiding facing your own deepest need.

+ Are you running away from life's biggest questions: Who am I? What is truth? What is the purpose of my life? What is worth living for?

+ Are you running away from reality by trying to satisfy the hunger of your soul with the candyfloss of "living it up."

The non-Christian is the escapist by refusing to look life (and death) straight in the eye. Have they got the courage to face the facts?

3 "When you leave God out, life becomes pointless - if you think logically"

If the universe began by chance, then it is governed by chance and is without purpose. This being so, our individual lives are meaningless also. As Fred Hoyle, the astronomer, wrote: "Here we are in a wholly fantastic universe with scarcely a clue as to the meaning of our existence."[12] If you think logically, what you believe about the origin of things affects radically the way you live today.

This is the dilemma of life in the modern world. We find it expressed in our art, films, literature and music. Jean-Paul Sartre, the French existentialist philosopher, wrote a play "No Exit"[13] - expressing that there is no way out of the human predicament. People have lost all hope of finding any ultimate meaning. There is a focus on the ephemeral, on transitory pleasure, excitement and entertainment as ends in themselves.

Challenge the person you are talking to with questions such as:

"What answer do you have for the deep emptiness of people today?"

"What would you offer to a drug-addict in place of their drugs?"

"What would you say to someone who felt life was worthless and wanted to commit suicide?"

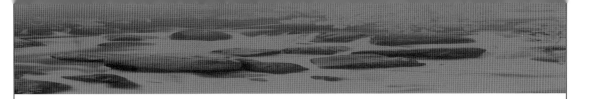

4 "Be a complete person"

We were made with a spiritual side to our nature so that we could relate to God and the spiritual world. So many today take good care of their bodies with food and exercise and of their minds with education. But the spiritual part of them is ignored. They are incomplete people. In fact, as the proverb says, "The good has become the enemy of the best." The good things that we enjoy in an affluent society have become the enemy of the best that comes through living contact with God. It is like someone who has filled his stomach with candyfloss and then passes by a steak because he has no appetite. God has made us to operate fully on every level of our personality - body, mind and spirit. Don't be content with less.

5 "How solid is your foundation for life?"

Is your happiness based on good health and good circumstances? If these go, have you got anything that will last? This makes us the slave and plaything of circumstances. We are not really free. Jesus Christ is the most solid foundation for life because he is *"the same yesterday and today and for ever"* (Hebrews 13:8). He offers us an abundant life that lifts us out of existence tied to our circumstances. Jesus said, *"I have come that they may have life, and have it to the full"* (John 10:10b).

6 "You don't want to lose your freedom. But the greatest slavery is to yourself"

Independence of God is a false freedom. We become tied to our own feelings, moods, ambitions, demands. We cannot escape even from our weaknesses. Personal ambition takes first place in our lives and we judge everything by how it affects us. "Everyone who sins is a slave to sin" (John 8:34).

True freedom comes by ending the stranglehold of self and becoming free to give ourselves in love to others and to Jesus Christ. "So if the Son sets you free, you will be free indeed" (John 8:36).

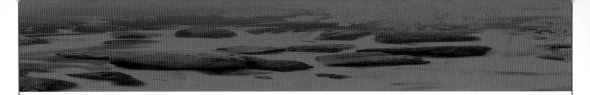

7 "Are you a scientist?
Then be scientific in your approach to Christianity" ——

People can pride themselves on their open-mindedness and clear thinking on subjects of scientific study and yet be prejudiced and sloppy when it comes to Christianity. Challenge them boldly to be open-minded and investigate the evidence thoughtfully, as they would their own field of study or knowledge. A scientist first observes the evidence, then draws a conclusion about it, and finally tests their conclusion by experiment to see if they are right.

Encourage and challenge your friend to study the evidence for Christianity. Good books would be "Case of the Empty Tomb" and "More Than a Carpenter" by Josh McDowell or "You Must Be Joking" and "Ten Myths about Christianity" by Michael Green.[14] They should come with an open mind and the prayer that God (if he is true) will help them to gain spiritual insight. Then they must come to a conclusion. But they will never be convinced until they have made the final "experiment", coming to God in repentance and faith to accept Jesus Christ.

8 "The most perfect man who ever lived depended on God more than anyone else has ever done" ———

To depend on God is not a sign of being a personality cripple. There has only been one flawless personality in history, Jesus Christ. If anyone did not need to depend on God it was him. Yet his dependence was total. *"The Son can do nothing by himself"* (John 5:19). Even if we too were perfect, we would still find our freedom in trusting and obeying God. But as we are far from perfect, if we are honest we will see our desperate need of him.

Point Two of "Knowing God Personally" explains that we were made for fellowship with God, but have turned to our own way. Machinery always works best when it operates according to the maker's instructions. To operate any other way is to limit ourselves.

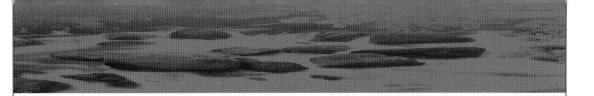

9 "People today have got themselves into a closed box, but are not happy to live there"

By misunderstanding science, humankind has come to believe in a closed system of cause and effect that has no place for the supernatural. Everything must be explained by natural causes without any outside interference. Only the scientifically provable is real. So thinking today is in a tightly closed box.

But people cannot happily live in such a confined space. They need the supernatural. But having rejected the supernaturally good, i.e. God, they are reaching out to the supernaturally evil. Hence the rise in popularity of black magic, seances, ouija boards, astrology, etc. "New Age" thinking is a reflection of this search to get in touch with the spiritual dimension of life. All this points to man's deep need of something above and beyond himself.

10 "Humanity's separation from God causes the world's problems"

Because of their sin and rebellion, humankind is faced with four separations each developing out of the other.

1 Separation from God

Genesis 3:10; Isaiah 59:2. Cut off from the Source of Life, death progressively spreads to every area of their existence.

2 Separation from nature

Genesis 3:17-19. Man and woman were given authority over the natural world in order to harmonise it and make it productive. But sin put them at odds with nature. From this have sprung our modern problems of thoughtless pollution, destruction of the environment, exhaustion of resources, etc.

3 Separation from one another

Genesis 4:8. Humankind soon fell into warring with each other as a result of envy, anger and competition.

4 Separation from oneself

Genesis 4:5,14. Inner turmoil follows with anger and fear. Our conflicts with others often spring from turbulent drives within us let loose by our rebellion against God (James 4:1).

Notes

1 **Josh McDowell,** *Evidence That Demands A Verdict, Volume I & II*
   (Thomas Nelson 1999)
   see also **Josh McDowell**, *Christianity, a Ready Defense*
   (Alpha 1991)

2 **Agapé,** *Knowing God Personally*
   (Birmingham: Agapé Ministries, 2001)

3 **Frank Morison,** *Who Moved The Stone?*
   (Lifestyle/Paternoster)

4 **Bertrand Russell,** *Why I Am Not A Christian*
   (London: Allen & Unwin, 1957)

5 **David Friedrich Strauss,** *The Life Of Jesus Christ Critically Examined*
   (London: SCM Press, 1973)
   Originally published as *Das Leben Jesu* (Tubingen, 1840)

6 *The Holy Bible, Revised Standard Version*
   (London: Thomas Nelson, 1952), p.v.

7 **Malcolm Muggeridge,** *Jesus Rediscovered*
   (Hodder & Stoughton 1995)

8 **C.S. Lewis,** *Mere Christianity*
   (Fount 1997)

9 **Catherine Marshall,** *To live Again*
   (Baker Book House of USA)

10 **Sigmund Freud,** *The Future of an Illusion*
   (Original paper, 1927) from The Standard Edition of the Complete
   Psychological Works of Sigmund Freud, Vol. XXI (London: Hogarth Press)

11 **Aldous Huxley,** *Ends and Means*
   (London: Chatto & Windus, 1969), p. 270.

12 **Fred Hoyle,** *Nature of the Universe*
   Broadcast talks (London: BBC, 1950)

13 **Jean-Paul Sartre,** *Husi-Clos*
   (Paris: Gallimard, 1945)

14 **Josh McDowell,** *The Case of the Empty Tomb*
   (Birmingham: Agapé Ministries, 1998)

   Josh McDowell, *More Than a Carpenter*
   (Kingsway 2001)

   Michael Green, *You Must Be Joking*
   (London: Hodder & Stoughton, 1992)

   Michael Green, *Ten Myths about Christianity*
   (Oxford: Lion pocketbook, 1988)

Appendix

The "Knowing God Personally" Booklet

Knowing God
personally

We live in a world where many are pessimistic
about the future. The media hype has done little to
persuade us that life will be better in the third
millennium. The problems of crime, violence,
economic uncertainty and human suffering show
little sign of going away. Against this background,
Jesus Christ offers real hope. He highlights our basic
need to find peace with God. He then makes such
reconciliation possible

THE FOLLOWING PAGES EXPLAIN HOW

1

GOD LOVES YOU

AND WANTS YOU TO KNOW HIM

HOW CAN YOU KNOW GOD LOVES YOU?
'God loved the people of this world so much that he gave his only
Son, so that everyone who has faith in him will have eternal life and
never really die.' *John 3:16*

WHAT IS ETERNAL LIFE?
'Eternal life is to know you, the only true God, and to know Jesus
Christ, the one you sent.' *John 17:3*

Why is it that most people do not know God in this way?

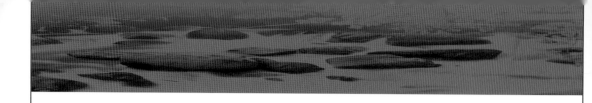

2

WE CHOOSE TO GO OUR OWN WAY,

CUTTING OURSELVES OFF FROM GOD

WE ARE EACH RESPONSIBLE

We prefer to go our own way instead of God's; we may openly disobey God who made us, or simply ignore him. It's this self-centred attitude that the Bible calls 'sin'.

WE ARE ALL THE SAME

'All of us have sinned and fallen short of God's glory.' Romans 3:23

WE EACH SUFFER THE EFFECTS

'That way of living leads to certain spiritual death.' Romans 8:13

God is perfect, we are sinful, so there is a great gap between us. We may try to feel better through work, relationships, sport or religion. But all our attempts fail, because we have ignored the real problem - turning our back on God.

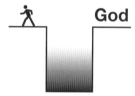

The third point gives us the only answer to this problem...

3

BY GIVING HIS LIFE FOR US, JESUS CHRIST OPENED

UP THE ONLY WAY TO FRIENDSHIP WITH GOD

JESUS IS UNIQUE

'I am the way, the truth and the life!' Jesus answered. 'Without me, no-one can go to the Father.' John 14:6

JESUS HAS THE POWER TO PUT THINGS RIGHT

'While we were his enemies, Christ reconciled us to God by dying for us.' Colossians 1:21,22

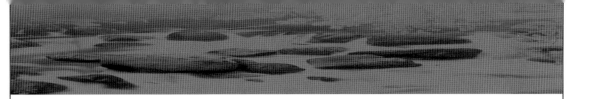

JESUS HAS POWER OVER DEATH

'For forty days after Jesus had suffered and died, he proved in many ways that he had been raised from death. He appeared to his apostles and spoke to them about God's kingdom.' *Acts 1:3*

Jesus took the consequences of our self-centredness by giving up his life on the cross. He proved he had broken sin's destructive power by rising from the dead. Jesus offers us freedom from guilt and a bridge back to God.

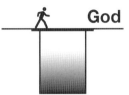

It's not enough just to know all this...

4

WE NEED TO ACCEPT JESUS CHRIST, SO WE CAN

KNOW GOD'S FORGIVENESS AND FRIENDSHIP

WE NEED TO ACCEPT JESUS CHRIST

'Some people accepted him and put their faith in him. So he gave them the right to be the children of God' *John 1:12*

ACCEPTING JESUS CHRIST INVOLVES:

1 Agreeing with God that we are to blame for turning our back on him
2 Trusting God to forgive us completely because Jesus has paid the price for our self-centredness
3 Choosing to follow Jesus

JESUS GIVES THIS PICTURE

'Listen! I am standing and knocking at your door. If you hear my voice and open the door, I will come in and we will eat together.' *Revelation 3:20*

It's not enough just to know or feel that these things are true. We have a choice to make...

These illustrations describe two kinds of people

 Self-centred person
- Self in the driving seat
- Jesus Christ outside
- Interests centred on self, often resulting in discord and frustration

 Christ-centred person
- Jesus Christ in the driving seat
- Self following Jesus Christ, drawing on his life and power
- Interests centred on Christ, resulting in growing harmony with God's purpose

Which illustration better describes you?
Which illustration would you like to describe you?

To accept Jesus Christ, you must put your life in his hands. God is not so concerned with your words as he is with your attitude. Here is something you could say to him:

'Lord Jesus, I am sorry that I have been going my own way. Thank you for paying the price of my self-centredness by dying on the cross. Please come and take first place in my life. Make me the kind of person you want me to be.'

Could you say this to God and mean it?

Why not say this to God now?
Jesus Christ will come into your life as he promised

WHAT HAPPENS WHEN YOU PUT

YOUR TRUST IN JESUS CHRIST?

If you have invited Jesus Christ into your life, many things have happened, including:

1. Jesus Christ has come into your life by his spirit and he will never leave you *Revelation 3:20; Hebrews 13:5*
2. You have been forgiven completely *Colossians 2:14*
3. You have a new power in your life, enabling you to change *Colossians 2:15*
4. You can begin to experience life with God as he intended *John 17:3; John 10:10*

HOW CAN YOU BE SURE

ALL THIS HAS REALLY HAPPENED?

You can know that Jesus Christ is in your life because God has promised and he can be trusted

'God has said that he gave us eternal life and that this life comes to us from his Son. And so, if we have God's Son, we have his life. But if we don't have the Son, we don't have this life. All of you have faith in the Son of God and I have written to let you know that you have eternal life.' *1 John 5:11-13*

'Thank God often that Jesus Christ is in your life and that he will never leave you.' *Romans 8:38,39*

You can know that the spirit of Christ lives in you and that you have eternal life from the moment you invited Christ into your life, because this is what he has promised.

Do not depend on how you feel

We can always rely on God and his promises in the Bible. But we cannot always rely on our feelings. Because of this, the Christian lives by trusting God and what he has said through the Bible, rather than by trusting feelings, which may come and go.

fact	faith	feeling
God and his word the Bible	Our trust in God and his word	The results of trusting God

It would be impossible for the guard's van to pull the train. In the same way, it is important to rely on God and what he has said in the Bible, and not be pushed around by our feelings. Just as the coal needs to be put into the engine from the coal truck in order for the train to run, so we need to put our trust in God's word.

SUGGESTIONS FOR CHRISTIAN GROWTH

OUR FAITH IN GOD GROWS AS WE TRUST GOD WITH EVERY DETAIL OF OUR LIVES. YOU WILL FIND IT HELPFUL TO:

- **G**et to know God by reading the Bible *2 Timothy 3:14-17*
- **R**espond to God in prayer *Philippians 4:6*
- **O**bey God moment by moment *Luke 6:46-49*
- **W**alk in the power of the Holy Spirit *Colossians 2:6; Ephesians 3:14-21, 5:18*
- **T**ell others about Jesus Christ by life and words *Matthew 28:18-20; 2 Corinthians 5:17-20; Ephesians 4:1*
- **H**ave contact with other Christians *Hebrews 10:25; Acts 2:42-47*

Several coals burn brightly together; but put one aside and its fire goes out. In the same way, it is very hard to live the Christian life by yourself. Go to a church where Jesus is worshipped and the Bible is taught, and join others who have come to know God personally and are growing in their relationship with him.

The "Knowing God Personally" booklet is published by and available from:
Agapé, Fairgate House, Kings Road, Tyelsey, Birmingham, B11 2AA.

Tel Sales: 0121 683 5090
Tel: 0121 765 4404
Fax: 0121 765 4065
Email: info@agape.org.uk
Web: www.agape.org.uk